The Digestive System

Injury, Illness, and Health

Revised and updated

Carol Ballard

Heinemann Library,
Chicago, Illinois

www.heinemannraintree.com
Visit our website to find out
more information about
Heinemann-Raintree books.

To order:

☎ Phone 888-454-2279
🖥 Visit www.heinemannraintree.com
to browse our catalog and order online.

©2003, 2009 Heinemann Library
an imprint of Capstone Global Library, LLC
Chicago, Illinois

Edited by Andrew Farrow, Adrian Vigliano, and
   Harriet Milles
Designed by Steven Mead and Geoff Ward
Original illustrations © Capstone Global Library Limited 2003
Illustrated by David Woodroffe and Geoff Ward
Picture research by Ruth Blair
Originated by Heinemann Library
Printed and bound in China by CTPS

13 12 11 10 09
10 9 8 7 6 5 4 3 2 1

Second edition ISBNs: 978 1 4329 3417 0 (hardcover)
                      978 1 4329 3430 9 (paperback)

**The Library of Congress has cataloged the first edition
as follows:**

Ballard, Carol.
  The digestive system / Carol Ballard.
    v. cm. -- (Body focus)
Includes bibliographical references and index.
Contents: The digestive system -- Chemical digestion --
Nutrition -- Problems with nutrition -- In the mouth -- Teeth -
- Esophagus -- Stomach -- Stomach problems -- Small intestine
-- Large intestine -- Intestinal problems -- Liver -- More about
the liver -- Pancreas -- Diabetes -- Kidney structure -- Kidney
function -- Kidney problems -- Bladder and urination.
  ISBN 1-40340-195-0 -- ISBN 1-40340-451-8 (pbk.)
 1. Digestive organs--Juvenile literature. 2. Digestion--Juvenile
literature. [1. Digestive system.] I. Title. II. Series.
  QP145 .B258 2003
  612.3--dc21
                        2002014420

Acknowledgments
The author and publishers are grateful to the following for
permission to reproduce copyright material: Corbis p. **16**;
Getty Images p. **15** (UHB Trust); Photodisc p. **10**; Science
Photo Library pp. **20** (J.C. Revy), **23** (Biophoto Associates),
24, **26** (Science Pictures), **27** (David M. Martin), **29** (Prof. P.
Motta/Dept. of Anatomy, University "La Sapienza," Rome), **30**,
31 (Dept. of Clinical Radiology, Salisbury District Hospital),
32 (Astrid & Hanns-Frieder Michler), **33** (Susumu Nishinaga),
35 (Ian Hooton), **40** (Richard J. Green), **41** (AJ Photo);
Shutterstock pp. **6** (Hannamariah), **9** (Marie C. Fields);
Rex Features p. **34**.

Cover photograph of large intestine X-ray reproduced with
permission of Science Photo Library (Athenais, ISM).

We would like to thank David Wright for his invaluable
help in the preparation of this book.

Contents

Words appearing in the text in bold, **like this**, are explained in the glossary.

The Digestive System

Our bodies cannot make use of the food we eat until it is broken down into smaller, **soluble** particles. This breaking-down process is called **digestion**, and the organs that carry it out are called the digestive system. The process happens automatically whenever we eat. Food is broken down, the particles of food are absorbed into the blood, and waste is removed from the body.

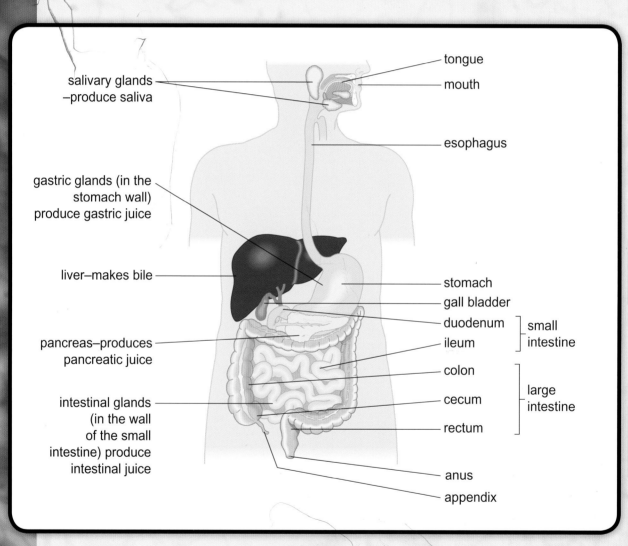

- tongue
- mouth
- salivary glands –produce saliva
- esophagus
- gastric glands (in the stomach wall) produce gastric juice
- liver–makes bile
- stomach
- gall bladder
- duodenum
- ileum
- small intestine
- pancreas–produces pancreatic juice
- colon
- large intestine
- intestinal glands (in the wall of the small intestine) produce intestinal juice
- cecum
- rectum
- anus
- appendix

↑ The digestive system processes the food we eat, so that our bodies can make use of the chemicals the food contains. This picture shows the main parts of the digestive system and other organs that are involved with the digestive process.

Food gives us energy, the building blocks for growth and repair, as well as the chemicals the body needs to stay fit and healthy. Eating the right amounts of the right types of food is important—eating too much or too little food can lead to health problems. Not eating a particular food type can also cause problems.

The digestive system is made up of a continuous tube from the mouth to the **anus** (called the alimentary canal) and other related organs. The alimentary canal begins with the teeth as we bite into our food. The teeth mash the food, and a liquid (**saliva**) in the mouth begins to digest it. Our sense of smell helps us to identify and savor what we are eating and to alert us to food that may be harmful. Our tongue contains millions of taste buds that allow us to distinguish many different flavors.

When we swallow, the soft food passes into a pipe called the esophagus, which carries it down to the stomach. Digestive juices in the stomach attack the food, breaking it down even more. The food, which is now a liquid, passes into a long, narrow tube called the small intestine. Here, more juices are added from the small intestine, liver, and **pancreas**. The particles that our body can use are absorbed into the blood, which carries them to every part of the body. Waste passes into the large intestine, where water is absorbed into the bloodstream, and the waste becomes drier and more solid. This solid waste, called **feces**, is stored in the rectum until we use the toilet, when it leaves the body via the anus.

Although not directly involved in digestion, other organs are important in processing the food we eat. The liver regulates the levels of sugars and other chemicals in the blood. The kidneys clean the blood, filtering out any waste chemicals and excess water. The bladder stores the liquid waste, called urine, until we use the toilet, when the urine leaves the body via a narrow tube called the urethra.

IN FOCUS: PHYSICAL AND CHEMICAL DIGESTION

Your food is digested in two main ways:

- Physical digestion happens when food is broken into smaller pieces by your teeth and tongue. Food is also broken down by the muscles in the gastrointestinal tract wall, which push food along the alimentary canal.

- Chemical digestion happens when enzymes and other chemicals break down the food at various stages, starting with the saliva in the mouth. This process is made easier because the food has been broken into smaller pieces by physical digestion.

Nutrition

The parts of food that our bodies can use are called **nutrients**. Different foods provide different nutrients. To stay healthy, we need to eat a variety of foods, in the right proportions, providing all the nutrients that we need—in other words, we need to eat a balanced diet. We can divide foods into six main groups:

1. *Bread, pasta, rice, flour, and cereals*: These contain **carbohydrates**, either as starches or as sugars. Unrefined carbohydrates, such as wholegrain cereals and whole wheat flour, also contain fiber, which helps the digestive system to function properly. They are of more value to the body than refined carbohydrates, such as white flour and white sugar, which contain little or no fiber. Our bodies use carbohydrates for energy.

2. *Vegetables*: These are important sources of **vitamins** and **minerals**, which are needed to maintain general good health. For example, vitamin A is needed for healthy skin and hair, and iron is needed for red blood cells to carry oxygen efficiently. Calcium, found in some leafy vegetables, is important for growth and maintenance of strong, healthy teeth and bones. Vegetables also provide fiber, which has no nutritional value, but is important in helping the digestive system to work efficiently. Fiber is the cellulose material that plant cell walls are made of. We are not able to digest this, so it adds bulk to the feces and makes it softer, which helps it to pass out of the body more quickly. Lack of fiber in the diet can lead to bowel problems.

3. *Fruits*: These are also important sources of vitamins and minerals. Citrus fruits, such as oranges and grapefruits, are rich in vitamin C, which helps to boost the **immune system**. Fruits also contain fiber, which helps the digestive system to function efficiently.

4. *Dairy products, such as milk, yogurt, butter, and cheese*: These are rich in **fats** that we use for energy. One gram of fat will give about 9 calories of energy. Dairy products are also good sources of calcium, as well as vitamins and **proteins**.

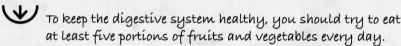 To keep the digestive system healthy, you should try to eat at least five portions of fruits and vegetables every day.

Foods for energy	Food	Energy—cal. in 100 g
Energy is measured in units called calories. We need to balance the amount of energy we use with the amount of energy we get from our food. Some foods contain more energy than others. This table compares the amount of energy in 100 grams of different types of food.	Apple	50
	Pasta	135
	Chicken	160
	Cheese	400
	Chocolate	500
	Salted peanuts	600
	Butter	720

5. *Meat, fish, eggs, nuts, and pulses*: These are good sources of proteins, which our bodies need for growing and for repairing damage. Proteins are made from smaller units called **amino acids**. The human body cannot make amino acids, but we can change some amino acids into others. However, there are at least eight amino acids (called essential amino acids) that we cannot make in this way, and so we have to obtain them from our food. It is easy to obtain all of them from animal sources, but vegetarians have to make sure that they eat a wide variety of different protein foods, as few of them contain all the essential amino acids.

6. *Fats and oils*: These are found naturally in many foods, and we often also add them to foods when serving or cooking. Some meats are very fatty, and cooking oils and many dairy products, such as butter, contain very little other than fat. These are good sources of energy and also provide important chemicals that the body needs for a variety of purposes. However, eating a lot of fatty food is bad for us, because the body stores excess fat.

Another essential part of a balanced diet is water. About 60 to 70 percent of a human body is water and, although we can survive for several weeks without food, we can only survive a few days without water.

HEALTH FOCUS: Malnutrition

Malnutrition occurs when a diet has not provided sufficient proteins or energy for a prolonged time. With too little protein and calories, muscle wastes away and growth is impaired. A diet rich in carbohydrates but lacking in protein leads to a swollen abdomen. Both types of malnutrition are common in children living in areas of the world affected by famine.

Chemical Digestion

Digestion is the process of breaking down food into smaller particles that can be used by the body. Different foods are digested in different ways, and in different parts of the digestive system. Food is digested physically into smaller pieces when we chew. As the food passes through the digestive system, chemicals digest the food into separate particles.

Enzymes

Enzymes are proteins that make chemical reactions happen. They act as catalysts—speeding up the reactions—but they do not get used up themselves. One enzyme can be used over and over again. Each enzyme is specific—it can only do one job.

Digestive enzymes break down large food **molecules** into much smaller units. There is a different type of enzyme for each type of food molecule. Enzyme names end with "ase," and the name usually gives some clue about what the enzyme does; for example, a protease breaks down proteins.

Proteins

Proteins are found in meats, fish, eggs, and nuts. They are very large molecules, made up of smaller units called amino acids. There are about 20 different amino acids in animal proteins. A small protein molecule might contain about 100 amino acid molecules, arranged in its own special order.

Protein digestion

The breaking down of proteins into single amino acids begins in the stomach. A protease enzyme breaks protein molecules down into smaller molecules called peptides. The pancreas, an organ that lies below the stomach, produces a liquid called pancreatic juice. This juice contains several more proteases and peptidases. It is added to the partly digested food in the small intestine, and its enzymes help to break down the peptides into individual amino acids.

Type of enzyme	Produced by	Action
amylase	salivary glands in mouth, pancreas	starch → maltose → glucose
protease and peptidase	stomach and pancreas	proteins → peptides → amino acids
lipase	pancreas	fats → fatty acids + glycerol

 This table shows where different enzymes are produced in the body, what they act on, and the molecules that are produced by this action.

 Foods such as breads and cakes are rich in carbohydrates.

Carbohydrates

Carbohydrates are found in foods that contain starch or sugar, such as bread, cereals, and pasta. They are made from a simple sugar called **glucose**. Two molecules of glucose joined together make another sugar, called maltose. Lots of glucose molecules can be joined together to make polysaccharides like **glycogen** or starch.

Carbohydrate digestion

Carbohydrates need to be broken down to give single glucose molecules. The digestion of starch begins in the mouth. Saliva contains an enzyme called salivary amylase that acts on starch and begins to break it down into maltose. When the maltose and any remaining starch reaches the small intestine, it is broken down into molecules of glucose by the pancreatic amylase and maltase in the ileum.

Fats

The scientific name for fats and oils is "lipids." One molecule of fat is made up from three smaller units, called **fatty acids**, and one unit of glycerol. Different fatty acids make up different fats.

Fat digestion

In the small intestine, **bile** (a liquid produced by the liver) is added to the partly digested food. Bile contains bile salts that break the fats down into small drops, to help speed up their digestion. These small drops are broken down even further by lipase, an enzyme in pancreatic juice, separating the molecules of fatty acids and glycerol.

Problems with Nutrition

If our diet does not provide all the nutrients we need, or if we eat more than we need, we will not be healthy.

Obesity

"Obesity" is the medical term for being very overweight. Although there can be other reasons for obesity, it is usually the result of eating too much and exercising too little. Being obese can lead to health problems, including heart disease and diabetes.

Body weight

If we take in the same amount of energy as we use, our weight will stay the same. If we take in more energy than we use, our weight will go up as our body stores the extra energy as fats or glycogen. If we take in less energy than we use, our weight will go down as our body uses up some of its store of fats or glycogen. It is important to try to keep a balance between the amount of food we eat and the amount of energy we use. Being very overweight or very underweight is bad for our overall health.

Eating disorders

Two common eating disorders are anorexia nervosa and bulimia. People who suffer from anorexia worry excessively about being overweight—even though they are usually very thin. People suffering from anorexia generally eat very little at meals or skip meals altogether. They may try to disguise how little they are eating by piling their plate with foods such as salad, which give them very little energy or protein. Friends and family may point out to them that they are already thin and need to eat more, but anorexic people are unable to believe them and continue to deny themselves food.

Junk food is often very high in fats and carbohydrates. It's fine to eat food like this occasionally, but eating it at every meal could lead to health problems.

HEALTH FOCUS: Using energy

The more active we are, the more energy we use up. We even use energy when we are sleeping. Our bodies use energy to maintain essential processes, such as heartbeat, breathing, brain function, and body temperature. The amount of energy food contains is usually measured in calories. In 24 hours, an average teenager might use almost 3,000 calories:

Activity	Hourly energy use	Energy used
8 hours asleep	70 calories	560 calories
8 hours awake but not active (for example, sitting reading or watching television)	100 calories	800 calories
8 hours physically active (for example, walking, playing soccer, swimming)	200 calories	1,600 calories
	Total energy used	2,960 cal.

Anorexics can cause great damage to their bodies. If the body does not get the nutrients it needs, it starts to use up muscle and organ tissue, leading to weakness, organ failure, and eventually even death. People with anorexia may need help from a doctor or specialist to re-establish a normal, healthy eating pattern. In severe cases, they may need to spend time at a residential treatment center or hospital.

People who suffer from bulimia also worry about being overweight. They may eat very little, then have a huge eating binge (bout of overeating), after which they make themselves vomit.

IN FOCUS: VITAMIN DEFICIENCIES

In the 18th century, sailors on long voyages had no fresh fruits or vegetables to eat. Many suffered from a disease called scurvy. It made their gums bleed and their teeth fall out. They became weak, their joints became swollen, and they usually died. Eventually it was found that giving them lime juice to drink kept them free from scurvy. Now we know that citrus fruits, such as limes, lemons, and oranges, contain high amounts of vitamin C, and that this prevents scurvy.

In the Mouth ...

Digestion begins when food enters the mouth. Teeth chew and soften food, and it is mixed with saliva. The tongue detects different tastes in the mouth.

Saliva

Saliva is a clear liquid made by the salivary glands in the mouth. There are three pairs of salivary glands in the mouth: one pair high at the sides and two pairs under the tongue. In an adult they produce more than 1 liter (2.1 pints) of saliva every day.

Saliva is neutral or slightly **alkaline**, which means that it is a base (the opposite of an **acid**) and can neutralize acids. Saliva helps to stop tooth decay by neutralizing the acids produced by **bacteria** in the mouth, preventing them from damaging the teeth. It also helps to keep the mouth moist and comfortable. It is about 99 percent water, but also contains **mucus**, mineral salts, and the enzyme salivary amylase. The mucus helps to make the food slippery and easy to swallow, and the salivary amylase begins the process of starch digestion.

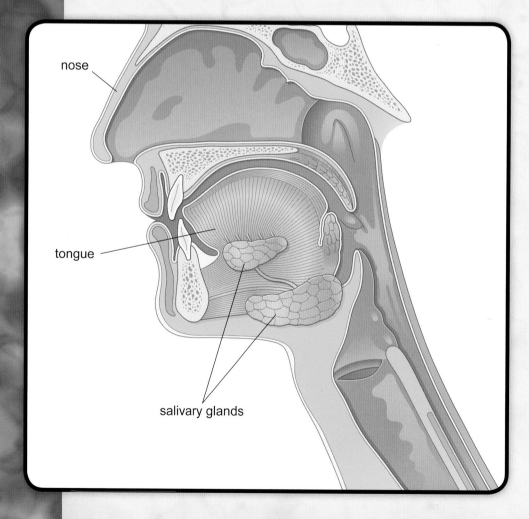

nose

tongue

salivary glands

In this diagram of the inside of the mouth, you can see the positions of the salivary glands.

This diagram shows the structure of a single taste bud. →

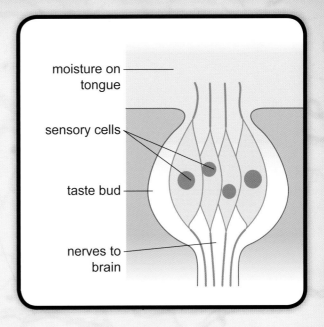

moisture on tongue

sensory cells

taste bud

nerves to brain

Taste

The tongue is mainly muscle. It helps to move food around the mouth when we chew, and it allows us to detect different tastes. In the upper surface of the tongue, taste-sensitive cells are clustered together in small groups called taste buds. As we chew, chemicals from our food touch our taste buds, and electrical signals are sent to the brain. Traditionally, four tastes have been identified—sweet, sour, salty, and bitter. Recently, scientists have identified a fifth taste, umami, which is found in foods such as meats and some cheeses and vegetables. They also think there may be taste receptors for chemicals such as calcium and some fats. Scientists used to think that each taste bud detected only a single taste. Recent research shows that it is not quite as simple as that: each taste bud can in fact detect more than one taste, but some areas of the tongue seem to be more sensitive to one type of taste than others. The tip of the tongue is most sensitive to sweet and salty tastes, the sides are most sensitive to sour tastes, the very back is most sensitive to bitter tastes, and the middle is most sensitive to umami.

Have you ever noticed that when you have a bad cold, your food seems less tasty than usual? This is because the nose also plays an important role in tasting our food. Cells that are sensitive to smells are situated in the upper lining of the nose. When chemicals in the air pass over the hairs of these cells, electrical signals are sent to the brain, adding information to the signals from the taste buds.

Swallowing

It can be painful if we swallow very hot or very cold food. As food is chewed, it gradually reaches the temperature of the body. When the food has been mixed with saliva and well chewed, it becomes soft and moist and is eventually ready to swallow. Several things happen:

● A flap of cartilage called the epiglottis blocks off the entrance to the windpipe, preventing food from entering the airways.
● The soft palate blocks off the entrance to the nasal cavity.
● The tongue pushes upward and backward against the roof of the mouth, pushing a small lump of food, called a **bolus**, to the back of the mouth.

We choose when we begin to swallow, but when the bolus hits the back of the mouth, swallowing becomes an automatic reaction. The food is forced out of the mouth and into the esophagus.

Teeth

Babies are born without teeth. The first set of teeth, called baby teeth or milk teeth, grow during the first year of life. During childhood, these gradually fall out and are replaced by permanent teeth. The last four molars, called wisdom teeth, often do not appear until the late teens; sometimes, they may never appear at all. Our teeth are very important, enabling us to take bites of food and to chew it for swallowing.

Baby teeth

The first teeth usually begin to appear before a baby is a year old. They continue to appear at the rate of about one pair each month, until there are 20 baby teeth altogether—10 in the upper jaw and 10 in the lower jaw. During early childhood, the permanent teeth slowly develop inside the gums. Between the ages of about 6 and 12 years, the permanent teeth are ready to emerge and the baby teeth are lost.

Permanent teeth

Adults have 32 teeth, 16 each in the upper and lower jaws. Each tooth has two parts: the crown is the part we see above the gum, and the root is hidden inside the gum. If these teeth are lost or damaged, the body cannot replace them.

Different shaped teeth do different jobs:
- Incisors at the front of the mouth are sharp and are good at snipping off pieces of food. We use these when taking a bite from a large piece of food such as an apple or cookie.
- Canine teeth at the side of the mouth are pointed. These are good for gripping and tearing food.
- Premolars and molars at the back of the mouth have large flat surfaces for crushing and grinding. We use these to chew our food, softening it and mixing it with saliva so it is ready to be swallowed.

Inside a tooth

Teeth are made up of several layers. The outer layer is a hard, shiny coating called enamel. Beneath this is dentine, a very hard layer like bone. The dentine obtains nutrients and oxygen from blood vessels that lie in the pulp (the soft core of the tooth). The pulp also contains nerves.

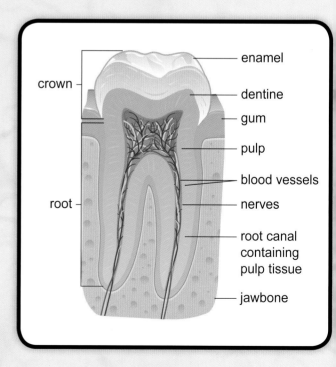

This diagram shows the internal structure of a tooth and the position of the tooth in the gum.

IN FOCUS:
TEETH AND DIET

The types of teeth we have give information about our diet. The large, sharp incisors of rodents, such as mice and squirrels, allow them to nibble at their diet of nuts and seeds. Carnivores, such as lions and foxes, have strong canines for gripping and tearing flesh. The flat molars of herbivores, such as sheep and horses, allow them to grind large quantities of plant material. Humans are omnivores, and so we have some teeth of each type to enable us to eat a mixed diet.

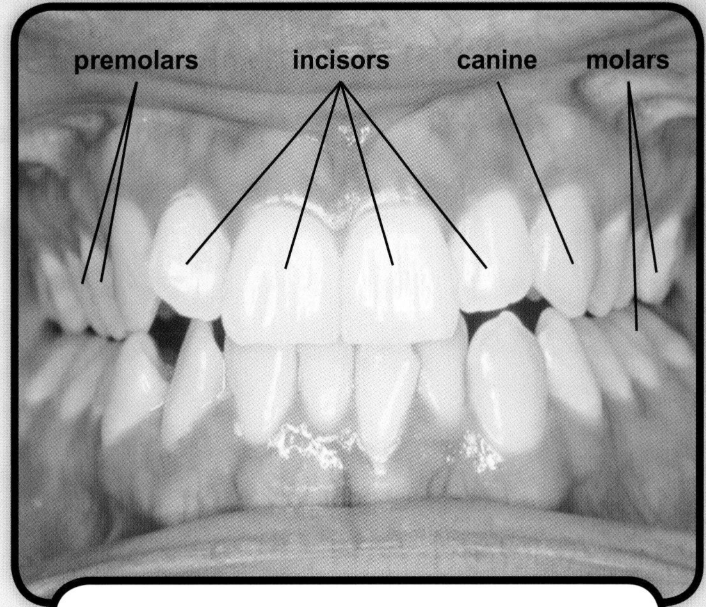

premolars   incisors   canine   molars

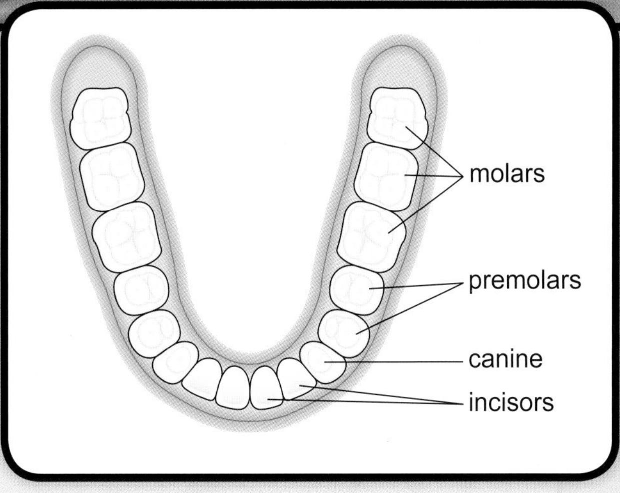

molars
premolars
canine
incisors

This diagram (right) shows the positions of the different types of teeth found in an adult mouth (top right). →

HEALTH FOCUS: Dental care

Our permanent teeth should last us for the rest of our lives. However, to do this they have to be taken care of. It makes sense to:

• remember to clean your teeth morning and night, as this helps to remove any scraps of food that remain and eliminate the bacteria that cause tooth decay

• avoid sugary, sticky foods, so that there is no sugar remaining on the teeth for harmful bacteria to feed on and produce damaging acid

• visit the dentist regularly, so that any problems are dealt with in the early stages, before tooth decay becomes too advanced.

Esophagus

The esophagus—sometimes called the gullet—carries food from the mouth to the stomach. In an adult it is about 25 centimeters (10 inches) long and has strong muscular walls that help to move the food along.

Trained sword swallowers like this one are able to control the natural reflex of the esophagus muscles, in order to pass the sword into their stomach. Sword swallowing is a life-threatening activity and should only be carried out by skilled, trained professionals. NEVER try this yourself.

The esophagus is made up of a series of layers. Although there are variations in size and surface details, the basic structure is the same throughout the alimentary canal.

1. The outer layer (adventitia or serosa) is a thin layer of connective tissue.

2. Beneath this is a layer of **longitudinal muscle** fibers that stretch the full length of the esophagus.

3. Next comes a layer of **circular muscle** fibers that run in rings around the esophagus.

4. Below this is a thick layer of connective tissue (submucosa) that contains nerves and blood vessels.

5. The innermost lining of the esophagus (**mucosa**) produces mucus that keeps the food slippery, helping it to slide easily along.

At the center of the esophagus is the space through which the food moves, called the lumen. Its irregular shape is made by the folds and wrinkles of the mucosa that surrounds it.

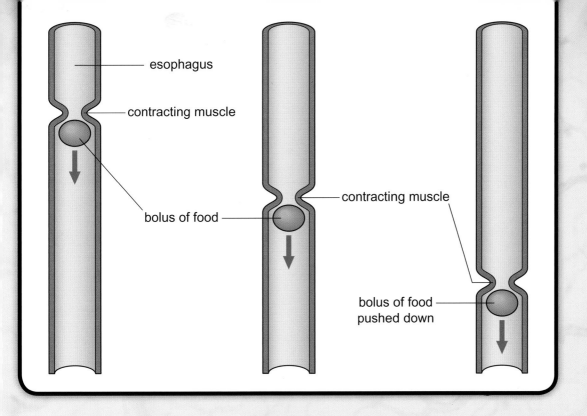

esophagus

contracting muscle

bolus of food

contracting muscle

bolus of food
pushed down

This diagram shows how muscle contractions push a bolus of food down the esophagus.

Moving food

Food cannot move along by itself. In the esophagus, muscles contract and relax in turn, pushing the food along. These muscle movements ripple along the esophagus like a wave. This process is called **peristalsis**, and it occurs at every stage along the alimentary canal.

The circular muscles behind the food contract, and the circular muscles in front of the food relax. This squeezes the bolus along a little way into the space where the muscles are relaxed. These muscles then contract, and the muscles in front relax—squeezing the food along again. The longitudinal muscles contract, too, so a section of the esophagus is shortened, helping to push the bolus forward. Food moves along the esophagus at about 4 centimeters (1.6 inches) per second, so it will take about six seconds to travel from your mouth to your stomach.

The pressure from the muscles is very high, so food is forced along the digestive system in the right direction—even if you are standing on your head! The bottom of the esophagus is kept tightly closed by a ring of muscle called the esophageal **sphincter**. It relaxes to allow food to enter the stomach and then contracts again to close the entrance to the stomach.

Gas

With every meal, we swallow air—sometimes as much as half a liter (1 pint). This may be released from the stomach by belching. Some may enter the small intestine and cause a gurgling sound as it travels along. Any remaining, excess gas leaves the body via the anus as flatulence, usually when we use the toilet.

Stomach

The stomach stores food from a meal. Digestive juices produced by the stomach break down the food, turning it into a liquid that is then passed on to the rest of the alimentary canal.

The stomach is a muscular sac that stretches to hold food from a meal. An adult's stomach is about 25 centimeters (10 inches) long and is made up of the same layers as the rest of the alimentary canal—a protective outer layer, longitudinal muscles, circular muscles, connective tissue, and mucosa. When the stomach is empty, the mucosa becomes wrinkled as it fills with food. These wrinkles gradually disappear, as the stomach stretches to hold the food.

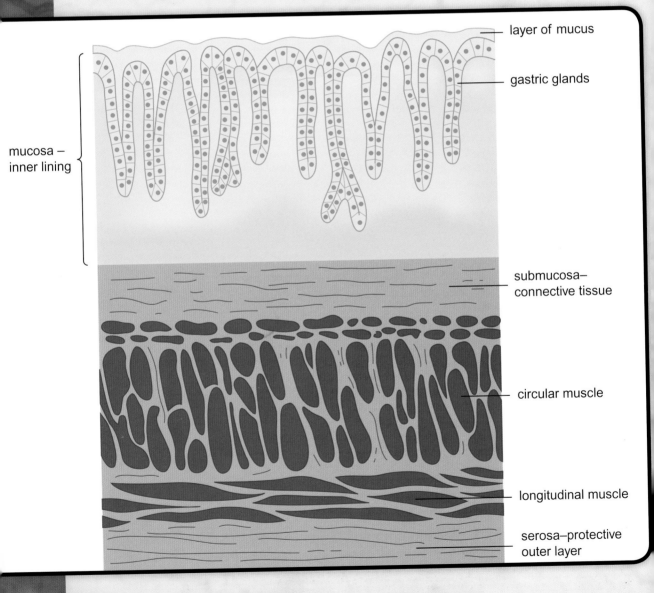

layer of mucus

gastric glands

mucosa – inner lining

submucosa– connective tissue

circular muscle

longitudinal muscle

serosa–protective outer layer

 This diagram shows the structure of the stomach wall.

The mucosa of the stomach contains special glands that make a liquid called **gastric** juice. About 1.5 liters (3.2 pints) is produced every day. Gastric juice contains:

- Pepsin: This is a type of protease, an enzyme that breaks down proteins into smaller molecules called peptides.
- Hydrochloric acid: Pepsin works best in acidic conditions, so hydrochloric acid is produced to keep the stomach contents acidic. The hydrochloric acid also helps to dissolve minerals and kill microorganisms.
- Lipase: This enzyme breaks down fats into fatty acids. However, because it is deactivated by the hydrochloric acid, little fat digestion takes place in the stomach, but occurs in the small intestine instead.
- Mucus: This helps to lubricate the food. Mucus also forms a protective layer covering the inside surface of the stomach, preventing it from being attacked by the acid and enzymes of gastric juice.

Churning food

When food enters the stomach, slow peristaltic waves start in the upper area of the stomach, with the muscles of the stomach wall contracting and relaxing about once every 20 seconds. These movements churn the food, mixing it thoroughly with the gastric juice. Different foods stay in the stomach for different lengths of time, depending on the chemicals they contain. Water passes through within a few minutes; a meal rich in carbohydrates, such as pasta, may pass through in less than an hour; meals containing fats and proteins, such as hamburgers and fries, may stay in the stomach for two to three hours.

The stomach churns and mixes the food, eventually turning it into a creamy liquid called **chyme**. The stomach does not absorb any nutrients from the food. The peristaltic movements of the stomach muscles squirt chyme out of the stomach via a ring of muscle, called the pyloric sphincter, and into the small intestine.

IN FOCUS: ALCOHOL AND THE STOMACH

Alcohol is not a nutrient. It can be absorbed into the bloodstream from both the stomach and the small intestine.

The stomach contains an enzyme that breaks down alcohol. Therefore, the longer alcohol stays in the stomach, the more it is broken down, and the less it is absorbed into the blood.

Drinking alcohol with a fatty meal, such as pizza and fries, gives the enzyme in the stomach more time to work. This also slows the rate at which the alcohol moves into the small intestine, where absorption is much more rapid than in the stomach.

Stomach Problems

Everything that we eat and drink passes through the stomach. Our modern diets and lifestyles can sometimes cause stomach problems, although there are often other causes, too.

Stomach ulcers

The thick layer of mucus lining the stomach usually protects it from attack by gastric juice. Sometimes, however, gastric juice can penetrate the mucus and damage the stomach wall. This damage is called a gastric ulcer. If the damage continues, blood vessels in the stomach wall may rupture, letting blood escape into the stomach. A perforated ulcer occurs if a gastric ulcer eats through the stomach wall, allowing food and digestive juices to escape into the abdomen.

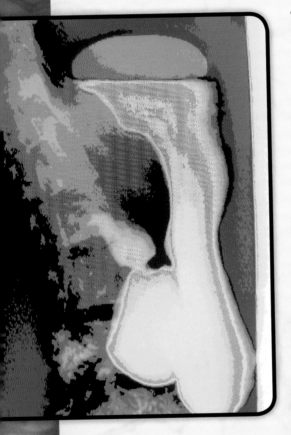

↑ X-rays cannot pass through barium sulfate; if a patient swallows a suspension of barium sulfate (a "barium meal"), the stomach (yellow/orange) can be seen clearly on an X-ray.

What causes ulcers?

A variety of things may lead to the development of a gastric ulcer. This includes smoking, drinking a lot of alcohol, eating irregular or hurried meals, and stress. It is unlikely that these would cause an ulcer on their own, but they may reduce the stomach's defense and repair mechanisms, making it susceptible to attack by its own hydrochloric acid. Some steroids and drugs, such as aspirin, may affect the lining of the stomach and increase the risk of developing a gastric ulcer. Australian scientists Barry J. Marshall and J. Robin Warren showed that most ulcers are caused by a bacterium, *Helicobacter pylori*, which produces chemicals that damage the stomach lining. This discovery earned them the Nobel Prize for Medicine in 2005.

Symptoms

A gastric ulcer usually causes pain in the upper abdomen and a sick feeling about an hour after a meal. Vomiting often helps to relieve the pain. To find out what is wrong, doctors can use an endoscope (a flexible fiber-optic tube that is passed down the throat and into the stomach) to examine the internal walls of the stomach. Alternatively, a barium X-ray can indicate the problem. Antacid tablets can ease the pain by neutralizing the stomach acid. A doctor can also prescribe drugs to reduce the amount of stomach acid produced, or to form a protective covering over the ulcer. Sometimes an operation is needed to repair the damage.

Untreated gastric ulcers may eventually begin to bleed, causing **anemia**. In very severe cases, they can be fatal.

Indigestion

Usually, the digestive system works without our being aware of it. Sometimes, though, we experience pain after eating a meal, together with a bloated, sick feeling. We call this indigestion; it is not dangerous and usually passes after a while.

Several things may cause indigestion. Particular foods, such as onions and cucumber, may lead to indigestion. These foods may remain in the stomach for longer than others, producing excess acid. In other cases, it may be due to overeating, eating hurriedly, stress, and drinking too much alcohol. Vomiting often gets rid of the pain, and antacid tablets can also help.

Heartburn

The esophageal sphincter usually remains tightly closed to prevent the stomach contents from moving back into the esophagus. Sometimes, however, the acid contents of the stomach do escape into the esophagus, causing a burning sensation as they irritate the lining of the esophagus. This is known as heartburn. It is not serious, and antacid tablets can relieve the pain.

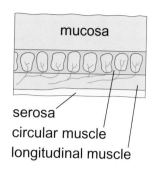

mucosa

stomach lining is healthy—mucus produced, protecting stomach wall

serosa
circular muscle
longitudinal muscle

ulcer beginning— mucus layer eroded

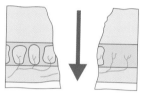

ulcer bleeding as stomach wall tissues eroded

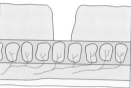

perforated ulcer— complete erosion of part of stomach wall

 These diagrams show how an ulcer may develop in the stomach.

IN FOCUS: VOMITING

Vomiting is the mechanism by which we can partly, or completely, empty the stomach. Several things happen when we vomit:

- The top of the stomach goes into spasm, and peristaltic waves start to operate in reverse, pushing food backward the wrong way along the alimentary canal.

- The body of the stomach and the esophageal sphincter relax.

- The upper part of the small intestine also goes into spasm, forcing its contents back into the stomach.

- The **glottis** closes; the soft palate raises to stop vomit from entering the airways.

- Abdominal pressure squeezes the stomach, forcing its contents back through the esophagus and out through the mouth.

Vomiting is the body's mechanism for getting rid of harmful substances, protecting it from poisons and infected foods. Too much vomiting can itself be damaging, though, leading to a dangerous loss of fluids and salts.

Small Intestine

The small intestine lies between the stomach and the large intestine. In an adult, it is about 3–4 centimeters (1½–1¾ inches) in diameter; its total length is more than 6 meters (20 feet), but muscles in the intestinal wall usually keep it contracted to about half this length. It is subdivided into three main areas: the duodenum, jejunum, and ileum. Food remains in the small intestine for between one and six hours. Digestion of food and absorption of nutrients takes place within the small intestine, leaving mainly waste matter to pass into the large intestine.

When the chyme leaves the stomach, it passes into the duodenum. This is about 25 centimeters (10 inches) long, and is shaped like the letter "C." In the duodenum, digestive juices from the liver and pancreas are added to the chyme:

- Bile is a watery, alkaline fluid made by the liver and stored in the gall bladder. It does not contain any enzymes, but bile salts act on fats to break them up into small droplets.
- Pancreatic juice from the pancreas contains several enzymes. Proteases break down proteins into peptides and amino acids. Pancreatic amylase digests starch, converting it into maltose. Lipase digests fats, breaking them down into fatty acids and **glycerol**. These enzymes do not work well in an acidic environment, so pancreatic juice also contains an alkali to neutralize the acid chyme.

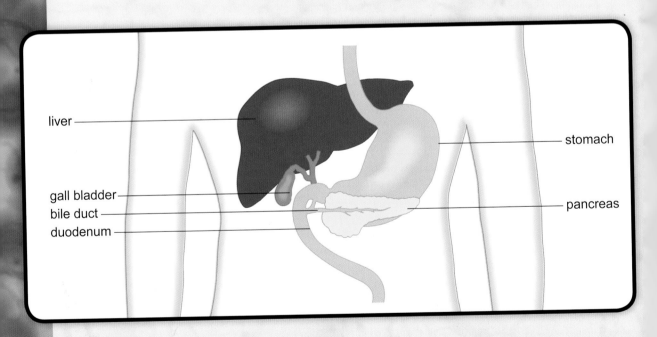

liver
stomach
gall bladder
bile duct
duodenum
pancreas

This diagram shows the duodenum and its connections with the bile duct.

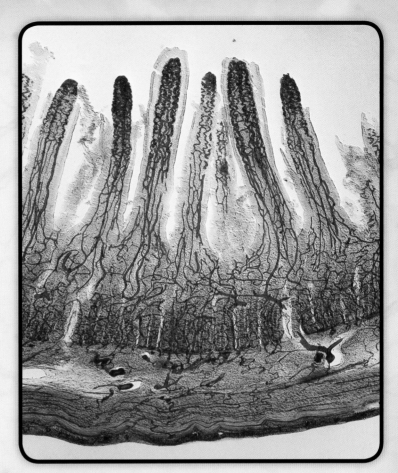

From the duodenum, the chyme passes into the jejunum (about 2.5 meters [8 feet] long) and then into the ileum (about 3.5 meters [11 feet] long). Glands in the walls of the small intestine produce a dilute mucus and salt solution for lubrication, and in order to provide a watery environment for the rest of the digestive processes to take place. Digestive enzymes are also produced by glands (called "crypts of Lieberkuhn") in the small intestine wall. These enzymes complete the breakdown of peptides into amino acids and of carbohydrates into simple sugars.

IN FOCUS: ABSORBING NUTRIENTS

Once food has been digested, it has to be absorbed into the body. The inner surface of the small intestine is well adapted to do this. Peristaltic waves, from the action of muscles in the intestine wall, move the food through the small intestine. The inner surface area of the mucosa has large, circular folds, each covered with tiny projections called "villi." Each villus is about 0.5 millimeters (0.02 inch) long and contains blood **capillaries** and a lymph vessel (a drainage tube, also called a lacteal). The outer edge of each villus is covered with thousands of smaller projections called microvilli. The folds (villi and microvilli) increase the surface area of the small intestine, providing about 600 times greater surface for absorption of nutrients than if it were flat. The walls of each villus are very thin, so that nutrient molecules can pass through them easily and quickly, mainly by the process of **diffusion**.

Sugars and amino acids pass from the villus into the blood capillaries and are carried away in the bloodstream. Fatty acids pass into the lacteal and are carried away into the **lymphatic system**. Water and minerals are also absorbed into the bloodstream—**water-soluble** vitamins enter the bloodstream and **fat-soluble** vitamins enter the lymphatic system.

After the absorption of nutrients, only waste matter and water is left. This passes into the large intestine.

Large Intestine

Liquid waste, from which nutrients have been absorbed, enters the large intestine. Water is removed in the large intestine, and solid waste passes on to the rectum, where it is stored until we use the toilet.

The large intestine is 1–1.5 meters (3.3–4.9 feet) long—one-sixth of the length of the small intestine. It is called the large intestine because it is about 6 centimeters (2.4 inches) in diameter, whereas the small intestine is less than 4 centimeters (1.6 inches) in diameter. Its main sections curve around to form the four sides of a rectangle, surrounding the small intestine.

Cecum

Liquid waste passes into the first section, the cecum, through a **valve** called the ileocecal sphincter. This is usually partly closed, allowing liquid through in a slow, steady trickle. The cecum is a short cul-de-sac, and its open end merges with the next section of the large intestine, the colon. Attached to the cecum is a small, narrow tube, called the appendix; this does not play any part in digestion, but may have some function as part of the body's immune system.

Colon

The next section of the large intestine is called the colon. The wall of the large intestine has no villi or folds, and no enzymes are produced. Absorptive cells absorb water from the waste, and goblet cells produce mucus for lubrication, helping waste slide easily along the large intestine.

Liquid waste is continuously pushed along the colon by slow peristaltic waves—between three and twelve each minute. The muscular walls of the colon generate these waves. Additionally, three or four times a day, usually during or after a meal, an extra-strong peristaltic wave sweeps along the colon, forcing the contents into the rectum.

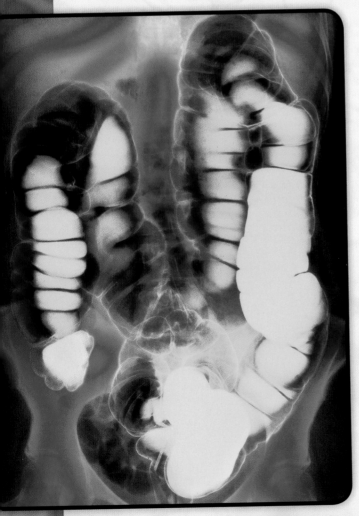

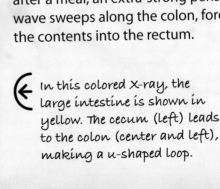

In this colored X-ray, the large intestine is shown in yellow. The cecum (left) leads to the colon (center and left), making a u-shaped loop.

This diagram shows how the main sections of the large intestine are curved into a rectangular shape. →

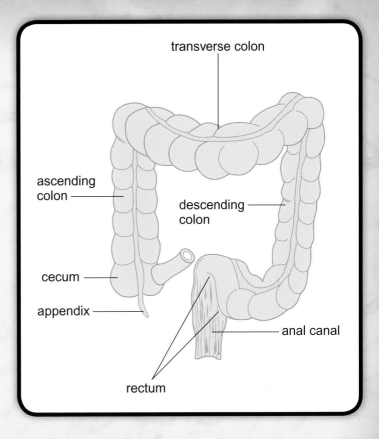

transverse colon

ascending colon

descending colon

cecum

appendix

anal canal

rectum

Although we generally think of bacteria as being harmful, we rely on the bacteria that live in the large intestine to complete the breakdown of waste. They convert any remaining carbohydrates and proteins into simpler substances and release some gases. Vitamins K and B12 are by-products of the action of bacteria and are absorbed into the blood.

Waste

Solid waste is called feces. It contains water, some minerals, waste products from blood and the intestinal walls, bacteria and bacterial products, unabsorbed material, and indigestible material such as fiber. An S-shaped bend leads from the end of the colon into the rectum. As feces collects in the rectum, the rectal walls stretch, stimulating stretch receptors in the wall. Rectal muscles contract, shortening the rectum and increasing the pressure inside. The feces pass into the anal canal, which has a rich network of blood vessels. At the end of the anal canal is the anus, ending in two sphincter muscles, both of which are usually closed. When we use the toilet, voluntary contraction of the diaphragm and abdominal muscles open the sphincters, and feces is pushed out of the body through the anus.

HEALTH FOCUS: Appendicitis

Any blockage in the appendix can lead to inflammation that we call appendicitis. It usually causes an uncomfortable feeling in the abdomen, which becomes severe. A hundred years ago, appendicitis was rare. Doctors think that it is becoming increasingly common because our diet generally contains much less fiber than that of previous generations. An operation to remove the appendix is usually carried out, to prevent the risk of the appendix bursting and spreading infection inside the abdomen. Because the appendix does not carry out any important function, we can live quite happily without it.

Intestinal Problems

Everybody has probably experienced an intestinal problem at some time. Some problems are mild and pass quickly, while others are more serious and may be long lasting.

Diarrhea

If waste moves through the large intestine too quickly, water cannot be absorbed. This results in watery feces and the uncontrollable need to use the toilet urgently. Diarrhea may be caused by infection from bacteria or a **virus**, often a result of eating food infected with a bacterium such as salmonella. It can also be caused by toxic substances, such as some weed killers, and sometimes by extreme nervousness.

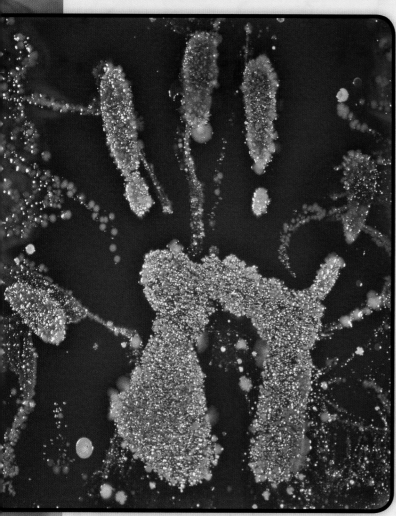

This handprint shows the bacteria that can develop if we do not wash our hands!

Diarrhea that continues for some time can lead to dehydration and loss of salts, because they pass through the alimentary canal too quickly to be absorbed. This is not usually serious in adults, but can be very dangerous in young children.

High standards of hygiene, both in food preparation and in personal behavior, such as washing your hands after using the bathroom, can help to reduce the risk of diarrhea from bacterial infection.

Constipation

If waste moves through the large intestine too slowly, too much water may be absorbed from it. This results in hard feces and difficulty in **defecation**. Constipation may be caused by a variety of factors, including a lack of fiber in the diet, too little exercise, stress, and some drugs. A mild laxative, which speeds up the movement of waste through the large intestine, may help to relieve the problem.

Inflammatory diseases

The intestine may become inflamed, giving a cramping pain and fever. If the inflammation is just in the large intestine, it is called ulcerative colitis; if it extends to other places in the alimentary canal, especially the ileum, it may be called Crohn's disease. A single cause has not been proved, but doctors think it may be due to an infection or **food allergy**. In mild cases, simple diarrhea remedies and vitamin supplements may be all that is needed. In more serious cases, drugs such as steroids may be given to suppress the immune system. Surgery to remove part of the bowel may be necessary.

Irritable Bowel Syndrome (IBS)

People suffering from IBS have alternating bouts of diarrhea and constipation, together with abdominal cramps and pains, a feeling of sickness, and loss of appetite. This condition is often associated with stress and depression. A change of diet can help, and drugs are available to control the symptoms.

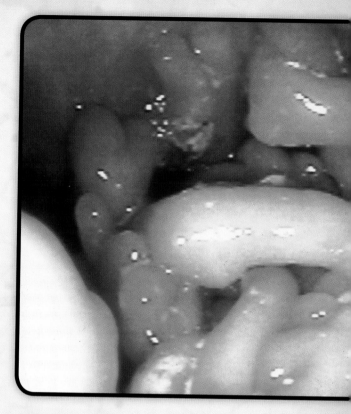

This photograph shows part of an intestine affected by Crohn's disease, which can seriously affect the digestive system.

Hernia

A hernia is a lump that arises when a loop of intestine protrudes through the abdominal wall lining. They are common and may be due to an inborn weakness, persistent cough (such as whooping cough or bronchitis), or the strain of lifting heavy objects. Hernias may be treated by surgical repair or by the wearing of a special belt.

Hemorrhoids

Sometimes called "piles," hemorrhoids are swellings that arise inside the anal canal. They are spongy tissues with a rich supply of blood vessels. As they get larger, they lead to bleeding and can be painful. The discomfort can be eased by a warm bath, and a high-fiber diet makes defecation easier. Treatment can be by injection to make the hemorrhoids shrivel, by freezing them, or by restricting their blood supply. An operation may sometimes be necessary to remove them completely.

Bowel cancer

Bowel cancer has become increasingly common, and many doctors think this is because our diets contain less fiber and more animal fat than in the past. It may cause diarrhea or constipation, bleeding from the rectum, and dull pain. If diagnosed in the early stages, many patients can be cured.

Liver

The liver is the largest organ in the body, with a mass of about 1.5 kilograms (3.3 pounds). It lies just below the diaphragm, a sheet of muscle that separates the chest from the abdomen. The liver has two lobes; the right (which is six times bigger than the left) lies in front of the right kidney. The liver is involved in the regulation and control of many of the body's systems.

Inside the liver
The liver is made up of many small areas called lobules. Each lobule has five or six sides and is about 1 millimeter in diameter. Blood and bile flow through the lobules in opposite directions.

Blood supply
Blood is brought to the liver in the **hepatic artery** and hepatic portal **vein**. The liver does not contain blood capillaries, but each lobule has a series of spaces through which the blood passes. Liver cells take up oxygen, nutrients, and toxic substances. The blood picks up products made by the liver and nutrients to be transported elsewhere in the body.

What does the liver do?
The conditions inside our bodies, such as temperature, chemical levels, and water level, need to be kept constant. The regulation of this internal environment is called homeostasis, and much of it is carried out by the liver.

This diagram ➜ shows the position of the liver in the body, and the blood vessels and organs that surround it.

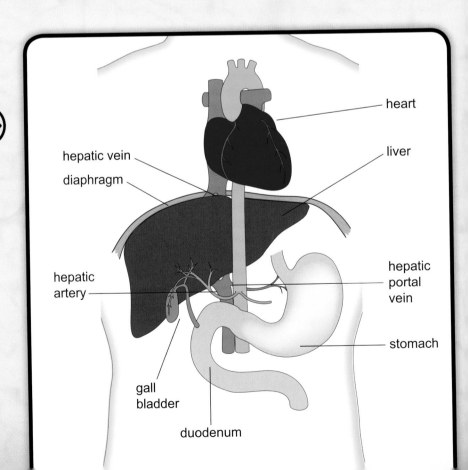

heart

hepatic vein

diaphragm

liver

hepatic artery

hepatic portal vein

stomach

gall bladder

duodenum

The main functions of the liver include:

- Regulation of blood sugar levels (the concentration of sugar in the blood): When the blood sugar level is high, the liver removes glucose from the blood and stores it as glycogen. When the blood sugar level drops, the reverse happens.

- Fat metabolism: The liver breaks down fatty acids and builds up new substances from them. Every day, the liver produces about 1 liter (2.1 pints) of bile, which is essential for the digestion of fats in the small intestine.

- Protein metabolism: When amino acids are broken down, ammonia is produced. Ammonia is toxic, and so the liver converts it into a harmless chemical, called urea, that is **excreted** in urine. The liver also produces some amino acids and proteins that are needed in the blood.

- Vitamins: The liver **synthesizes** vitamin A from carotene, a chemical found in some fruits and vegetables, especially carrots. The liver also activates vitamin D and stores many other vitamins until they are needed.

- Minerals: The liver removes iron from the **hemoglobin** of broken-down red blood cells and stores it until it can be used to make new red blood cells; hemoglobin is essential for oxygen to be transported. The liver also stores other minerals until they are needed.

- Toxins: Harmful chemicals, such as alcohol, drugs, poisons, environmental pollutants, and surplus **hormones**, are removed from the blood and broken down by enzymes in the liver.

- Temperature control: The many chemical reactions that are carried out inside the liver generate heat. This warms the blood as it passes through, and the blood carries the heat to the rest of the body, helping to maintain a constant body temperature.

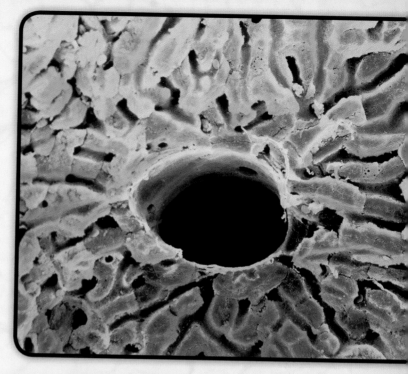

This is a greatly magnified image of a lobule of the liver.

Gall bladder

The gall bladder is a small, pear-shaped organ that lies under a lobe of the liver. It stores bile and makes it more concentrated by absorbing water from it. The gall bladder also produces mucus for lubrication.

Liver Problems

The liver is a complex organ, continuously carrying out a large variety of chemical reactions. It carries out essential functions without which the body would not survive, but it can be damaged by poisons, drugs, and infections.

Cirrhosis

Cirrhosis is a chronic liver disease, in that normal liver cells are destroyed and replaced by fibrous tissue that makes the liver hard and unable to function efficiently. In the early stages there may be no symptoms, but as the disease progresses, hormones may accumulate as the liver fails to break them down, and **jaundice** may occur as bile builds up in the blood. The abdomen may swell, body muscles become weak, and there may be internal bleeding. Eventually the circulation in the liver is blocked, leading to liver failure and death. The most common cause of cirrhosis is heavy consumption of alcohol over a long period of time. The liver is, however, able to repair itself, as long as it is not too badly damaged. If cirrhosis is detected at an early stage, and the patient stops drinking alcohol, the damage can be repaired.

Hepatitis

Hepatitis is usually caused by a viral infection, resulting in inflammation of the liver. It can affect people of all ages and is highly infectious. There are three main types: A, B, and C.

Hepatitis A is often spread in contaminated food or water. It is usually a mild disease, causing no long-term problems.

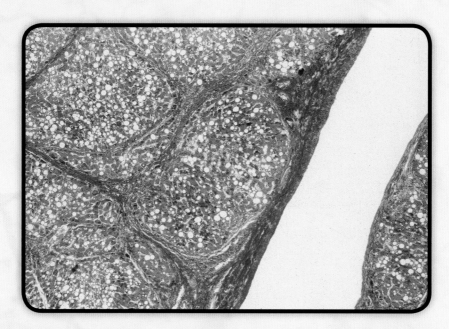

 Fibrous scar tissue (green) has developed around the lobules in this patient's liver. This damage has been caused by too much alcohol.

Hepatitis B and Hepatitis C may be spread in infected blood, and they can also be spread sexually. They are common among drug addicts who may share hypodermic needles. Babies of infected pregnant women may also be infected.

In most cases, infection by Hepatitis A or B is mild and may not even be noticed, although blood tests can detect the infection and indicate which virus is involved. More severe infections can result in jaundice, with recovery within a few weeks. In some cases, the infection persists and the liver is permanently damaged.

Treatment of hepatitis includes rest and a diet rich in carbohydrates, but low in fat.

Jaundice

When old red blood cells are broken down and the yellow bile pigment is released, it is usually removed from the blood by the liver. It is then excreted from the liver in bile, and the levels of bile pigment in the blood are normally very low. If the amounts in the blood rise, the skin becomes a yellow color and the patient may feel more tired than usual. This is known as jaundice, and it is common in newborn babies, when the liver is not mature enough to cope with the breakdown of red blood cells.

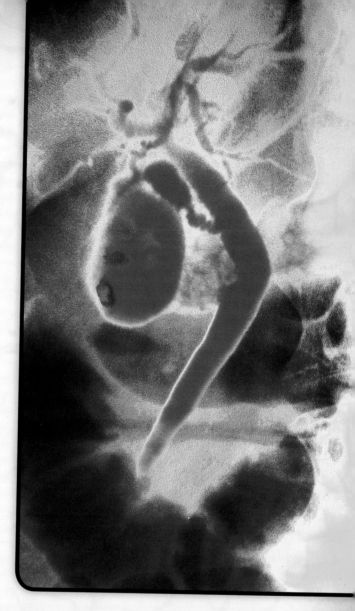

This X-ray shows that the patient's gall bladder (red, pear-shaped) contains many gallstones (green).

Gallstones

If there is too much cholesterol (fatty substance) in the bile, or not enough bile salts, the cholesterol may crystallize, forming gallstones. Initially, these may not cause any problems, but as they get bigger they may block the bile duct. Bile cannot leave the gall bladder, so fat digestion is impaired and jaundice may occur. In some cases, eating a fat-free diet can control the problem. Alternatively, gallstones can be treated with drugs to dissolve them or by lithotripsy (shockwaves) to shatter them. They may also be surgically removed, and in some patients the entire gall bladder may be removed. After treatment, the patient can resume a perfectly normal life.

Pancreas

Just behind the stomach lies a small, pinkish-gray organ called the pancreas. This produces pancreatic juice containing important digestive enzymes. It also produces hormones, including **insulin** and **glucagon**, which help to regulate the amount of sugar in the blood.

In an adult, the pancreas is about 12–15 centimeters (4.7–5.9 inches) long and 2.5 centimeters (1 inch) thick. The cells of the pancreas need a good blood supply to allow them to function and to carry away the hormones they produce.

When taste buds in the mouth detect food, messages are sent to the brain; in turn, the brain sends messages to the pancreas, stimulating the production of pancreatic juice in preparation for digestion of the food.

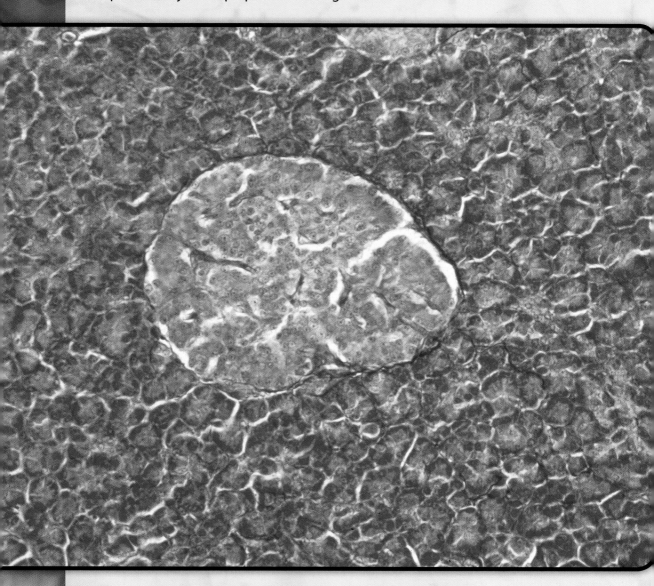

This magnified image shows how the endocrine cells inside the pancreas are arranged in an islet of Langerhans.

The majority of cells in the pancreas are exocrine cells. Here, they have been greatly magnified.

Pancreatic cells

There are two main types of cell in the pancreas: exocrine cells and endocrine cells.

About 99 percent of the pancreatic cells are exocrine cells. These are arranged in groups, and they produce pancreatic juice. They are clustered together around tiny ducts, which form a network to carry the pancreatic juice away. These ducts eventually join together to form two large ducts. The bigger of these is the pancreatic duct. This joins the common bile duct from the gall bladder and liver, and carries pancreatic juice and bile to the duodenum (part of the small intestine). The smaller of the two ducts is the accessory duct, which leads straight from the pancreas into the duodenum, about 2–3 centimeters (0.8–1.2 inches) higher than the pancreatic duct.

The other 1 percent of cells in the pancreas are endocrine cells. These cells are clustered together into small groups called islets of Langerhans. There are two different types of cell in each islet, each producing a different hormone that is released into the blood.

These hormones interact with each other, and this interaction helps to regulate the amounts of each that are produced. Blood components and intestinal contents also play a part in regulating the production of these hormones.

Diabetes

There are several types of diabetes, all of which lead to the inability to control blood sugar levels. It is a major cause of death in developed countries, more because of its side effects than the disorder itself.

Controlling blood sugar levels

Blood sugar levels are controlled by the interaction of the liver and pancreas.

The pancreas produces two hormones: insulin and glucagon. If the level of sugar in the blood begins to drop, the pancreas produces glucagon. This enters the blood and is carried to the liver, where it stimulates liver cells to convert some of their stored glycogen into glucose. This is released into the blood, and the blood sugar level returns to normal.

If the amount of sugar in the blood rises above normal, the pancreas produces insulin. It enters the blood and is carried to the liver, where it stimulates liver cells to remove glucose from the blood and store it as glycogen. This reduces the blood sugar level.

This feedback system operates effectively to maintain the blood sugar level within the correct limits. In patients with diabetes, the system does not operate, and they are therefore unable to control their blood sugar levels.

Types of diabetes

There are two main types of diabetes.

 Despite being diabetic, rower Steve Redgrave has won five Olympic gold medals. Diabetes should not stop anyone from taking part in sports.

- *Type I (insulin-dependent) diabetes*
  This usually begins before the age of 20 and continues throughout the rest of the patient's life. One of the main causes is the immune system attacking and destroying the cells in the pancreas, preventing insulin production. Excess glucose builds up in the blood and is excreted in the urine; the patient may produce up to 20 liters (42 pints) of urine a day and needs to drink a lot of water to replace this fluid. The body behaves as if it is starving. Waste products called ketones build up in the blood and make the blood more acidic—if untreated, this may eventually cause death. Regular injections of insulin, to lower blood sugar level and compensate for sugar intake, prevent this from happening.

  Side effects of Type I diabetes include thirst, weight loss, heart and blood problems, loss of vision, and kidney damage.

- *Type II (non-insulin dependent) diabetes*
  Type II diabetes accounts for 90 percent of diabetics. It usually affects overweight people over the age of 35. Patients have plenty of insulin, but their cells have become less sensitive to it and so cannot remove sugar from the blood. The symptoms are milder than those of Type I; some patients may need insulin injections, but in many the high glucose levels are controllable by a low-sugar diet, regular exercise, and weight loss.

Other blood sugar disorders are less common and may have a variety of causes. These include:

- *Hyperinsulinism (also hypoglycemia)*
  This can occur if a patient injects too much insulin. The blood sugar level falls too low, and brain cells do not have enough glucose to function normally. Within minutes, the patient feels shaky and, unless glucose is given quickly, will become unconscious and may die.
- *Hyperglycemia*
  Hyperglycemia can occur if a patient's blood sugar level rises too high. It is a much slower process than hypoglycemia, taking several hours to develop, and several hours to get back to normal.

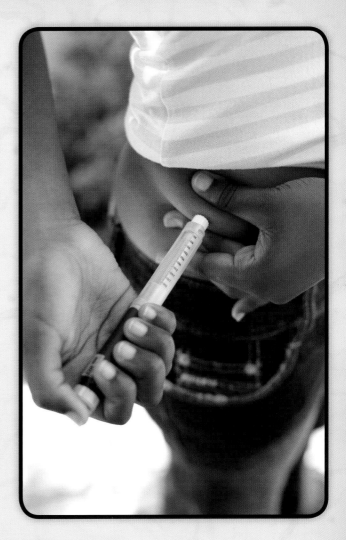

Type I diabetics lack insulin, so they need to inject it regularly.

HEALTH FOCUS: Living with diabetes

Although the outlook for diabetics has improved dramatically, it is still not an easy condition to live with. Controlling the blood sugar level requires careful discipline, and this can be very frustrating, especially if you are a teenager just wanting to be the same as your friends. A dietician can help you plan what to eat and what to avoid—reducing fats, avoiding sugar and salt, and eating regular meals are all important. The amount of food you take in must be carefully balanced with the amount of exercise that you get. Doctors will give instructions about how often the blood or urine should be tested to show the sugar levels, and about how much insulin must be injected and how often.

Kidneys

We have two kidneys, which are reddish organs, each about 10–12 centimeters (3.9–4.7 inches) long and about 5 centimeters (2 inches) wide. There is one on each side of the spine just above the waist, and they are partly protected by the lower ribs. The right kidney is a little lower than the left, because the liver takes up some abdominal space on the right of the body. Their main function is to filter the blood, removing waste chemicals and water, and producing a liquid, called urine, that is passed to the bladder. Having filtered out unwanted chemicals, the kidneys then pass back salts, other chemicals, and water to the blood, ensuring that the right level of each is maintained.

Blood supply

In order to filter the blood, the kidneys need a good blood supply. Blood travels to each kidney via the **renal arteries** and leaves via the renal veins. Inside the kidney, the arteries branch many times to form a network of smaller vessels. Approximately 1.2 liters (2.5 pints) of blood flows through the kidneys every minute. All the blood in the body passes through the kidneys about 340 times every day!

Together, the kidneys are able to filter more blood than the body actually needs them to. A single kidney is able to filter enough blood on its own. We can survive and live a healthy, active life with just one kidney.

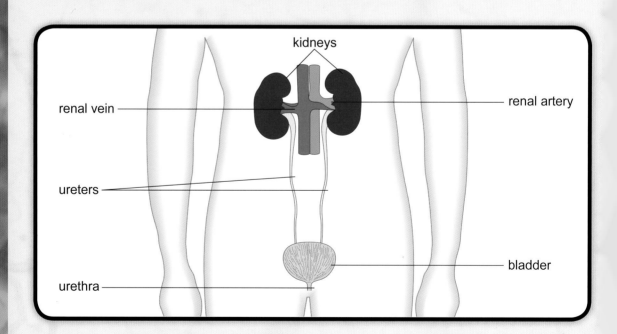

We have two kidneys, one on either side of the spine, above the waist.

This diagram shows the internal structure of a kidney. →

Kidney structure

Each kidney has a transparent outer membrane that anchors it to the abdominal wall. Below this is a layer of fat that acts as a cushion to protect the kidney from damage.

If a kidney is cut in half from top to bottom, three different areas can be seen:

- At the center of the kidney is a large space called the pelvis. This is where urine collects. The pelvis is connected to a narrow tube called a ureter, along which urine flows from the kidney to the bladder.
- The middle part of the kidney is a pale area called the medulla. This is made up of 8 to 18 cone-shaped areas and contains ducts that carry urine to the pelvis.
- The darker outer layer, the cortex, is where the blood is filtered. Here, the renal arteries branch into smaller vessels called arterioles. Each arteriole leads to a glomerulus, a group of blood vessels coiled around into a knot. Around each glomerulus is a renal capsule (sometimes called a Bowman's capsule) leading to a renal tubule. These eventually join collecting ducts that pass through the medulla, opening into the pelvis at the top of a pyramid shape. The cortex of a kidney contains thousands of glomeruli. One glomerulus, with its renal capsule, tubule, and blood capillaries, is called a nephron.

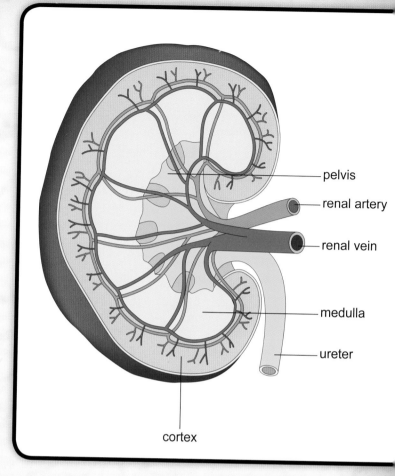

pelvis

renal artery

renal vein

medulla

ureter

cortex

IN FOCUS: KIDNEY TRANSPLANT

A patient's diseased kidney may be removed and replaced with a healthy one from another person. Drugs need to be taken to ensure that the patient's body does not reject the new kidney. Unfortunately, the waiting list for kidneys is long, and patients may wait many years before a suitable kidney becomes available.

What Happens in the Kidneys?

A nephron consists of a single glomerulus together with its blood capillaries, renal capsule, and renal tubule. It is here that the basic functions of the kidney are carried out. Blood is filtered, unwanted substances are removed, and useful substances are returned to the blood. This maintains the correct levels of fluid and chemicals in the blood and produces urine, so that waste can leave the body.

Ultra-filtration

The glomerulus and its capillaries are the places where ultra-filtration occurs. This is the process by which substances are removed from the blood.

Blood enters the glomerulus via a capillary. The capillary leaving the glomerulus is narrower than the one entering it, so the pressure inside the glomerulus is raised. This forces fluid out of the blood through the capillary wall. Blood cells and plasma proteins are retained, since they are too large to pass through the capillary wall. The fluid that passes out by diffusion is mainly water and dissolved salts, glucose, urea, and uric acid. This fluid collects in the renal capsule.

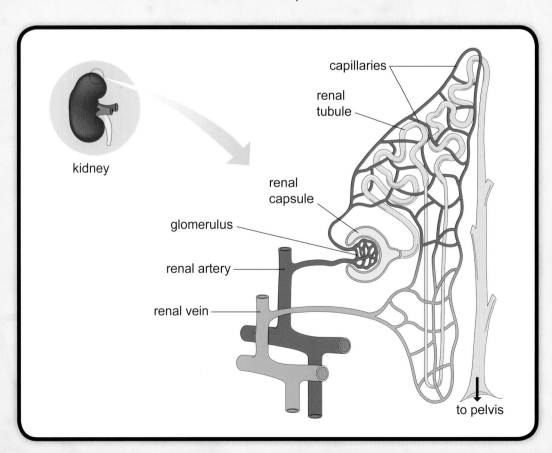

kidney

capillaries

renal tubule

renal capsule

glomerulus

renal artery

renal vein

to pelvis

These pictures show what the internal structure of a kidney is like, when magnified.

Selective reabsorption

Selective reabsorption is the process by which substances are added back to the blood. It takes place as the fluid collected in the renal capsule trickles down the renal tubule.

As the fluid flows through the tubule, substances that the body needs are absorbed back into the blood. Water, glucose, and some salts are taken back, to maintain the correct levels in the blood. The fluid then passes through the collecting duct and eventually to the pelvis of the kidney, before it leaves the kidney via the ureter.

Urine production

Any water and salts not needed by the body pass on down the tubule, together with urea and uric acid. They enter the renal tubule and collect in the pelvis of the kidney, forming the liquid we call urine.

How much urine?

Normally, we produce about 1–1.5 liters (2.1–3.2 pints) of urine every day. This is affected by the amount of water we drink and the amount that we sweat. If we drink a lot, we produce a lot of urine. The amount of chemicals to be filtered out remains the same, so the urine is very dilute. If we sweat a lot, we produce much less urine. Again, there is still the same amount of chemicals to be filtered out, so the urine is more concentrated. Some substances, such as caffeine and alcohol, are diuretics—they increase the amount of urine produced. Dilute urine is a very pale, almost colorless liquid. The more concentrated it is, the darker and stronger the color.

IN FOCUS: URINE TESTS

Urine can contain different amounts of different substances, and this can provide important information about your health. Any glucose in the urine can be a sign of diabetes, while the presence of protein in urine may be a sign of kidney failure. Pregnancy tests detect a hormone (human chorionic gonadotrophin, HCG) that is produced by a fertilized egg and excreted in the mother's urine eight days after conception.

Kidney Problems

There is a variety of things that can affect the efficient functioning of the kidneys. Some problems may affect just one kidney, while other problems may affect both. If one kidney fails, the other is usually able to cope with the extra work. If both fail, a patient has to rely on mechanical methods to clean the blood.

Kidney stones

Kidney stones are formed when crystals of salts present in urine solidify into **insoluble** lumps. If they settle in narrow tubes, such as the ureters, they can cause violent, stabbing pains. Kidney stones can be surgically removed, but a newer, alternative technique for their removal is "shock wave lithotripsy." This involves brief, high-intensity sound waves fired at the stones, eventually shattering them into tiny fragments, which are carried away in the urine.

Bacterial infections

Bacterial infections can affect any of the tissues of the kidneys. They are most commonly caused by bacteria such as *Escherichia coli* (E.coli), a bacterium that is usually present in the intestines, spreading from the bladder to the ureters and then into the kidneys. Treatment with **antibiotics** usually brings the infection under control quickly.

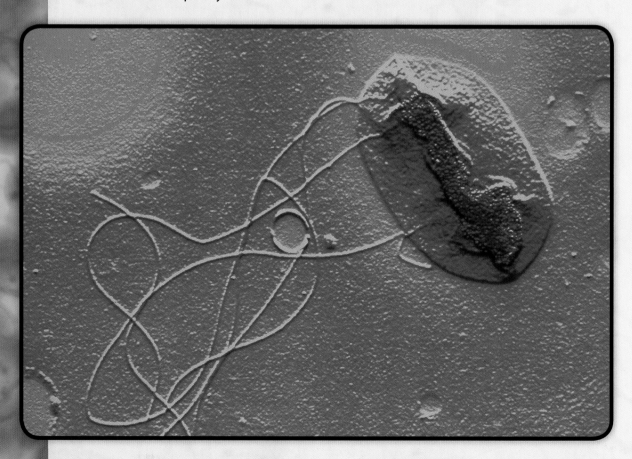

 This image shows the E.coli bacterium, which can cause kidney infections.

Cancer of the kidney

Cancer of the kidney is much more common in men than in women and occurs most often between the ages of 50 and 60. If detected in the early stages, treatment may be by surgery to remove the kidney, followed by **radiotherapy** and **chemotherapy**. However, the cancer often spreads to other parts of the body, making treatment less successful.

Floating kidney

If a kidney is not attached to the back of the abdomen, it is free to move around inside the abdomen—this is called a "floating kidney." It can be caused by sudden, extreme twisting movements, and it may twist the ureter, making it difficult or impossible to pass urine.

Kidney defects

Some people are born with kidney defects. These include having only one kidney, two kidneys fused together, two ureters from each kidney, cysts inside the kidneys, and kidneys in the wrong place within the abdomen. Each individual case is different; some may need treatment, while others will not cause any problems and may go unnoticed for years.

This patient has been linked to a dialysis machine to cleanse her blood.

Kidney failure

Kidney failure may be sudden (acute), or it may slowly develop over several years (chronic). There are a variety of causes, including heart attack, buildup of toxic chemicals, kidney blockage, and kidney inflammation. There are a wide range of symptoms, but the main symptom is a significant reduction in urine production.

IN FOCUS: TREATING KIDNEY FAILURE WITH DIALYSIS

Blood must be cleansed, and if a patient's kidneys are unable to perform the task, a dialysis machine (or "artificial kidney") may be used. This pumps blood from an artery through a series of tubes made from a special membrane. A solution called dialysis fluid is on the other side of the membrane, and as blood passes along, the salts and waste products move out of the blood by diffusion, through the membrane and into the dialysis fluid. The cleansed blood then goes back to the body. Each cycle of dialysis takes several hours, and most patients need treatment two or three times every week. While many patients undergo dialysis at a hospital, some have dialysis equipment at home, which makes it much easier for them to continue with work and other everyday activities.

Bladder and Urination

The bladder is a sac that collects urine from the kidneys and holds it until we use the toilet. Urine contains waste products, and urination is an efficient method of removing them from the body.

Ureters

The ureters are narrow tubes that carry urine from the kidneys to the bladder. Each ureter is between 25–30 centimeters (9.8–11.8 inches) long and between 1–10 millimeters (0.04–0.4 inches) in diameter. Urine is forced along the ureters by peristaltic waves, one to five times every minute, depending on how fast urine is being produced.

The ureters enter the bladder, one at each side. Before they open to the inside of the bladder, they run at an oblique (slanted) angle for a short distance as they pass through the bladder wall; this acts as a check valve, allowing urine to flow into the bladder but preventing it from flowing backward.

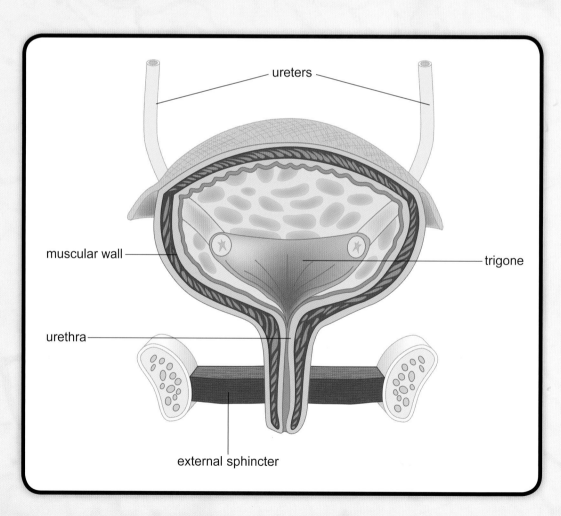

 This diagram shows the internal structure of the bladder.

Bladder

The bladder is a hollow, stretchy organ, held in place by the folds of the **peritoneum**. Its shape depends on how much urine it contains: if it is empty, it is collapsed, like an empty balloon; when partly full, it is spherical; when completely full, it is pear-shaped.

Urethra

The urethra is a tube of smooth muscle that carries urine from the bladder to outside the body. It is about 4 centimeters (1.6 inches) long in a female, running from the bladder and opening just in front of the vagina. In males, the urethra is about 20 centimeters (7.9 inches) long, running from the bladder along the length of the penis, to open at the tip of the penis. A ring of muscle around the urethra (a sphincter) controls the release of urine from the body.

Urination

On average, an adult's bladder can hold 700–800 milliliters (23.7–27.1 fluid ounces) of urine, but we usually feel more comfortable emptying it when it is about half-full. When the bladder contains 300–400 milliliters (10.1–13.5 fluid ounces) of urine, the pressure inside it increases. Stretch receptors in the bladder wall send signals to the spinal cord, triggering a reflex reaction. This makes muscles in the bladder wall contract, and the urethral sphincter relaxes. Urine is forced out of the bladder and through the urethra.

As children, we learn to control this reflex, and we can delay urination for a limited period.

Incontinence

Incontinence is the inability to control the reflex reaction in the bladder wall. In babies and very young children, incontinence is normal because they have not yet learned to control the reflex reaction. Adults may also suffer from incontinence, often as a result of physical stresses—coughing, sneezing, laughing, exercising, and pregnancy—that can increase abdominal pressure and cause leakage from the bladder. It can also be caused by physical injury, aging, disease, and the effects of some drugs.

HEALTH FOCUS: Cystitis

Cystitis is inflammation of the bladder. It is usually caused by the bacterium *Escherichia coli* (E.coli) and is much more common in women than in men. The first sign is a tingling or burning sensation when urinating, which gradually gets worse and more painful. Treatment may be with antibiotics to kill the bacteria. Drinking plenty of water to flush out the bladder, eating a healthy diet, and good personal hygiene can all help to reduce the likelihood of cystitis occurring.

What Can Go Wrong with My Digestive System?

This book has explained the different parts of the digestive system, why it is important, and how it can be damaged by injury and illness. The table below summarizes some of the problems that can affect young people. It also gives you information about treating each problem and tells you some of the ways you can prevent injury and illness.

Illness or injury	Cause	Symptoms	Prevention	Treatment
tooth decay	damage to teeth by acid from bacteria in the mouth	toothache, mild at first, but developing to severe pain if untreated	calcium-rich diet—for example, plenty of milk. Avoid sweets and sugary foods and drinks. Maintain good dental hygiene, brushing and flossing teeth twice a day. Have regular dental checkups.	cleaning of tooth and drilling out damaged tooth tissue. Replacement with plastic or metal material. In severe cases, removal of the tooth may be necessary.
indigestion	overeating, eating too quickly, eating particular foods (such as cucumber or onion), stress	pain after a meal and a bloated, sick feeling	eat smaller meals, eat more slowly, and avoid foods that are likely to cause indigestion. Reduce stress.	vomiting gets rid of excess or problem food. Antacid tablets can reduce the acidity of the stomach contents.
diarrhea	bacterial and viral infection, toxic substances, extreme nervousness	watery feces, an uncontrollable need to use the toilet urgently	maintain high standards of personal hygiene, such as always washing hands after using the toilet. Prepare and store food hygienically.	drink water to replace lost fluid. Antibiotics may help to clear up an infection. Ingestion of toxic substances may require urgent medical treatment.
irritable bowel syndrome	stress or depression, lack of fiber in the diet	bouts of diarrhea and constipation, abdominal cramps and pains, sickness, loss of appetite	reduce stress. Change diet to include more fiber by eating more fruits and vegetables.	some drugs can help to control the symptoms
constipation	too little exercise, stress, lack of fiber in the diet	hard feces, making it difficult to use the toilet	increase exercise and reduce stress, change diet to include more fiber by eating more fruits and vegetables	a mild laxative can help to move waste through the large intestine more quickly, easing the problem

Many health problems can also be avoided by healthy behavior. This is called prevention. Exercising regularly and getting plenty of rest are important, as is eating a balanced diet. A balanced diet is particularly important for maintaining a healthy digestive system.

Remember, if you think something is wrong with your body, you should always talk to a trained medical professional, like a doctor or a school nurse. Regular medical checkups are an important part of maintaining a healthy body.

Find Out More

Books to read

Ballard, Carol. *Food for Feeling Healthy* (*Making Healthy Food Choices*). Chicago: Heinemann Library, 2007.

Jakab, Cheryl. *Digestive System* (*Our Body*). Mankato, Minn.: Smart Apple Media, 2007.

Parker, Steve. *Break It Down: The Digestive System* (*Freestyle: Body Talk*). Chicago: Raintree, 2007.

Websites to visit

http://kidshealth.org/teen/nutrition/general/digestive_system.html
This website for young people offers information about the digestive system and healthy eating.

www.imcpl.org/kids/guides/health/digestivesystem.html
This library website offers information about the digestive system.

www.mypyramid.gov
This U.S. Department of Agriculture website provides information about the MyPyramid guidelines for healthy eating.

www.diabetes.org
This website of the American Diabetes Assoication provides information about diabetes and its treatment.

www.kidney.org
This website of the National Kidney Foundation provides information about kidneys and kidney problems.

Glossary

acid liquid that is sour to taste, can eat away metals, and is neutralized by alkalis and bases

alkali opposite of acid

amino acid one of the basic units of a protein molecule

anemia lack of hemoglobin in the blood

antibiotic drug used to destroy harmful bacteria and fungi

anus opening through which solid waste leaves the body

artery large blood vessel carrying blood away from the heart

bacteria group of microorganisms that can cause infections

bile liquid produced by the liver that helps to break down fats

bolus lump of food that is swallowed

capillary very fine blood vessel that links arteries and veins

carbohydrate nutrient that can be broken down to release energy

chemotherapy treatment of disease, especially cancer, by the use of chemical substances

chyme partly digested liquid food that leaves the stomach

circular muscles muscles arranged in rings

defecation removal of solid waste from the body

diffusion movement of molecules from an area of high concentration to an area of low concentration

digestion process of breaking food down into smaller units

enzyme protein that acts as a catalyst in chemical reactions. A catalyst speeds up chemical reactions.

excrete get rid of waste substances

fat substance that stores and releases energy

fat-soluble can be dissolved in oils

fatty acid one of the basic units of a fat molecule

feces solid waste material that leaves the body

food allergy sensitivity to a particular food that may lead to an allergic reaction

gastric to do with the stomach

glottis space between the vocal cords at the top of the larynx

glucagon hormone produced by the pancreas

glucose sugar that stores and releases energy

glycerol substance that combines with fatty acids to make fats

glycogen sugar that can be stored by the body

hemoglobin red pigment found in red blood cells that transports oxygen around the body

hepatic to do with the liver

hormone chemical made in the body. Hormones travel around the body in the blood and affect organs and tissues in a variety of ways.

immune system body's defense mechanisms against infection and disease

insoluble will not dissolve

insulin hormone produced by the pancreas

jaundice condition in which the skin turns yellowish as excess bile pigments build up in the blood

longitudinal muscles muscles that run straight up and down

lymphatic system system of drainage vessels, also involved in the body's immune responses

mineral one of a number of chemicals needed by the body in very small amounts—for example, calcium and iron

molecule tiny particle of a chemical

mucosa layer of tissue that produces mucus

mucus sticky, slimy fluid that acts as a lubricant

nutrient part of our food that the body can use

pancreas abdominal organ that produces insulin and other hormones

peristalsis wave motion of muscles that pushes food along the alimentary canal

peritoneum membrane lining the abdominal cavity and covering the organs within it

protein type of large molecule that makes up some of the basic structures of all living things

radiotherapy treatment of disease, especially cancer, by the use of X-rays or similar radiation

renal to do with the kidneys

saliva digestive juice made by salivary glands in the mouth

soluble able to dissolve in a liquid

sphincter ring of muscle that closes an opening

synthesis making something new

valve mechanism for controlling the flow of a liquid through a tube

vein large blood vessel carrying blood back to the heart

virus very small microorganism that can cause infection

vitamin one of a number of complex chemicals that the body needs

water-soluble can be dissolved in water

Index